DR. FAUCI

SIMON & SCHUSTER BOOKS FOR YOUNG READERS
An imprint of Simon & Schuster Children's Publishing Division
1230 Avenue of the Americas, New York, New York 10020
Text © 2021 by Kate Messner
Illustration © 2021 by Alexandra Bye
Book design by Chloë Foglia © 2021 by Simon & Schuster, Inc.
SIMON & SCHUSTER BOOKS FOR YOUNG READERS and related marks
are trademarks of Simon & Schuster, Inc.
For information about special discounts for bulk purchases, please contact Simon & Schuster Special Sales at
1-866-506-1949 or business@simonandschuster.com.
The Simon & Schuster Speakers Bureau can bring authors to your live event. For more information or to
book an event, contact the Simon & Schuster Speakers Bureau at 1-866-248-3049 or visit our website at
www.simonspeakers.com.
The text for this book was set in Caxon.
The illustrations for this book were rendered digitally.
Manufactured in the United States of America
0521 PHE
First Edition
2 4 6 8 10 9 7 5 3 1
Library of Congress Cataloging-in-Publication Data
Names: Messner, Kate, author. | Bye, Alexandra, illustrator.
Title: Dr. Fauci : how a boy from Brooklyn became America's doctor / Kate Messner ; illustrated by
Alexandra Bye.
Description: New York : Simon & Schuster Books for Young Readers, 2021. | Audience: Ages 4–8 | Audience:
Grades K–1 | Summary: "Before he was Dr. Fauci, director of the National Institute of Allergy and Infectious
Diseases, Anthony Fauci was a curious boy in Brooklyn, delivering prescriptions from his father's pharmacy
on his blue Schwinn bicycle. His father and immigrant grandfather taught Anthony to ask questions,
consider all the data, and never give up—and Anthony's ability to stay curious and to communicate with
people would serve him his entire life. This engaging narrative, which draws from interviews the author
did with Dr. Fauci himself, follows Anthony from his Brooklyn beginnings through medical school and his
challenging role working with seven US presidents to tackle some of the biggest public health challenges of
the past fifty years, including the COVID-19 pandemic. Extensive back matter rounds out Dr. Fauci's story
with a time line, recommended reading, a full spread of facts about vaccines and how they work,
and Dr. Fauci's own tips for future scientists"— Provided by publisher.
Identifiers: LCCN 2021009196 | ISBN 9781665902434 (hardcover) | ISBN 9781665902441 (ebook)
Subjects: LCSH: Fauci, Anthony S., 1940-—Health. | Physicians—Juvenile literature. | Physicians—United
States—Interviews—Juvenile literature. | Physicians—Biography—Juvenile literature. | Medical care—United
States—History—Juvenile literature.
Classification: LCC R153 .M47 2021 | DDC 610.92 [B]—dc23
LC record available at https://lccn.loc.gov/2021009196

DR. FAUCI

HOW A BOY FROM BROOKLYN BECAME AMERICA'S DOCTOR

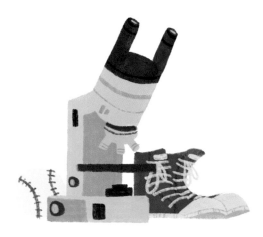

BY
KATE MESSNER

ILLUSTRATED BY
ALEXANDRA BYE

SIMON & SCHUSTER BOOKS FOR YOUNG READERS
NEW YORK   LONDON   TORONTO   SYDNEY   NEW DELHI

Anthony Fauci was always asking questions, wondering about the world. From the tropical fish in his bedroom aquarium . . .

to the vast oceans of sea life, the blazing stars, and the spinning planets in the pictures of his encyclopedias. How did it all work? With a wide-open mind, Anthony searched for answers.

His family encouraged that curiosity.

When the nuns at his school said you had to go to Mass each week in order to get into heaven, Anthony wondered about his grandfather, an Italian immigrant who spent his Sundays over steaming pots of pasta and bubbling red sauce. Anthony asked his grandfather why he didn't go to church.

"When I make you all the good food, that's my Mass," his grandfather answered, "so don't worry about me. I'm going to be fine."

Anthony's dad ran a drugstore. While his mom and older sister served customers at the cash register, Anthony zipped around the neighborhood on his Schwinn bicycle, delivering prescriptions. Sometimes he'd get a nickel for a tip!

Fauci PHARMACY

Anytime Anthony struggled with homework, his father reminded him that every problem has a solution.

"DON'T GET discouraged. DON'T RUN AWAY BECAUSE YOU DON'T UNDERSTAND THE PROBLEM. THINK ABOUT IT carefully AND try TO WORK IT OUT."

Anthony learned to start with wondering, then gather evidence and keep an open mind.

His neighborhood was full of tough guys, and Anthony wasn't that big. But he learned to get along with everyone. He was good at talking to people, and listening, too.

The boys compared notes about their favorite baseball players and played stickball in the streets. Who could hit the ball the farthest? They measured by sewers—really, by the manhole covers that led down to the city sewers, spaced about a hundred feet apart. If you hit the ball past one sewer, you were pretty good. But two sewers? That was impressive. Anthony was proud to be a two-sewer guy.

Anthony loved basketball, too, but he was shorter than the other players. How could he compete? He thought about that problem and realized the solution was speed. He couldn't shoot the ball over his opponents, but he could dash past them. One of his teammates said he was so quick, he could dribble through a brick wall!

Anthony might have been short, but the other guys looked up to him. They admired his determination and the way he could talk to everyone, so they chose Anthony to be captain of the team.

In high school Anthony realized he wanted to be a doctor. He went to college and got a summer job working construction to help pay for his tuition. When the crew was building a new library for the Cornell medical college in New York City, Anthony snuck inside to peek at the grand auditorium. What would it be like to learn in such an extraordinary place?

Then a guard showed up. Anthony's work boots were tracking mud all over the floor! Anthony told the guard that he was going to attend medical school there in a year. The guard laughed and asked him to leave. So Anthony left . . . but not for long.

He attended that medical school and graduated first in his class. Now he was Dr. Fauci!

He became one of the country's top experts on what makes people sick . . . and how to make them well.

Soon Dr. Fauci had a whole country of people to care for, a new team to lead, and a lot of problems to solve. It was good that he'd learned how to get along with all different kinds of people back in Brooklyn. His job required that.

New diseases were emerging. Germs no one had seen before were making people sick. Dr. Fauci and his researchers had to gather evidence and keep an open mind. They searched and studied, and did a lot of listening.

When a deadly disease called AIDS began spreading through the United States, people criticized government leaders for not doing enough to stop it.

AIDS PROTEST

"WE NEED RESEARCH — NOT HYSTERIA"

ACT UD

LEGALIZE AIDS PREVENTION

AIDS

HEALTH CARE IS A RIGH

WE NEED HEALTHCARE NOT BIGOTRY

SILENCE DEATH

NO

Protesters chanted and shouted outside Dr. Fauci's office. He invited some of them inside to talk so they could work together to find solutions.

Every new disease was a mystery to wonder about, a problem to solve. Where had it come from? How did it spread? How could it be prevented until researchers found a cure or a vaccine?

EBOLA

2014

One of Dr. Fauci's biggest challenges came when a new disease appeared at the end of 2019—COVID-19, caused by a coronavirus. Within weeks, the virus spread around the globe.

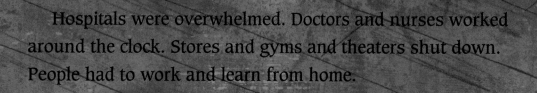

Hospitals were overwhelmed. Doctors and nurses worked around the clock. Stores and gyms and theaters shut down. People had to work and learn from home.

A virus too tiny to see had stopped
the whole world in its tracks. Where had
it come from? Why was it spreading so
quickly? How could anyone stay safe?

People wanted answers—and at first Dr. Fauci simply didn't have them. More and more people got sick.
But there had to be a solution.

DON'T GET discouraged. THINK ABOUT IT carefully. Try TO WORK IT OUT.

Dr. Fauci kept an open mind. He worked with scientists around the world. They listened to one another, gathered evidence, and searched for solutions. They shared ideas, discovered new information, and revised those ideas. They taught people simple ways to be safe while researchers developed medicines and a vaccine.

Within a year, people began rolling up their sleeves for the shots that would protect them, so they could go back to school, back to work, back to hugging their families and playing with their friends.

Dr. Fauci did that too.

Through all those months of problem-solving, he'd looked forward to being together with his family again, making good food and sharing stories. Soon enough, it would be time to get back to work . . .

searching for solutions to whatever
challenges might come next.

HOW DO VACCINES WORK?

When germs such as bacteria and viruses invade your body and multiply, they can make you sick. But the good news is, you have a built-in collection of disease-fighting superpowers! It's called your immune system.

Your body, like all living things, is made up of tiny building blocks called cells, and some of those cells help fight disease. Some special blood cells swallow up germs. Others produce antibodies, which are special proteins that also help fight germs. After your body battles an infection, it remembers how to protect you against that particular disease. But when a new germ shows up, your immune system might take a while to start attacking it.

Vaccines help by teaching your immune system how to fight specific germs before you even encounter them. Sometimes vaccines introduce a dead version of the germ, a harmless piece of it, or a code that gives instructions so your own cells can create part of the germ. That tricks your body into thinking it's been infected, so your immune system will be ready to go when the real germ shows up.

Vaccines aren't medicine. They don't kill germs; they boost your body's natural disease-fighting superpowers so that you can fight the germs off yourself.

ARE VACCINES SAFE?

Vaccines like the ones developed for COVID-19 are very safe. Before vaccines are used on people, scientists do many tests to make sure the vaccines will help fight disease and won't cause harm. When researchers develop a new vaccine, they test it on laboratory animals such as mice first. If the vaccine seems to work, then the scientists do a series of tests on human volunteers, in several stages.

Phase 1: Researchers give the vaccine to a small number of volunteers to make sure it's safe. The scientists study how well the vaccine works and what size dose is needed.

Phase 2: Scientists give the vaccine to *hundreds* of volunteers of different ages and backgrounds to find out if it works well on everyone. These tests also confirm that the vaccine is safe.

Phase 3: Researchers give the vaccine to *thousands* of volunteers to learn how well it protects against disease. Scientists also check *again* to make sure the vaccine is safe.

Approval: After all that testing, a new group of scientists reviews the results. When all those experts decide the vaccine is safe and good at preventing illness, they approve it and make it available to everyone.

Did you know . . . when you roll up your sleeve for a vaccine, it doesn't protect only you? By boosting your immune system to fight disease, you also help to make sure you won't spread germs to your family, friends, or community. Getting a vaccine makes *you* a disease-fighting superhero!

DR. FAUCI'S FIVE TIPS FOR FUTURE SCIENTISTS

By Dr. Anthony Fauci

Photo credit: NIAID

1. Keep an open mind. Science is discovery, which means that from the beginning, you don't know what the answer is. Leave open all the possibilities of what you might find.

2. **Don't be afraid to fail.** In science you fail more often than you succeed. So don't get discouraged by something that doesn't work. Ultimately that's what science is all about. It's step-by-step learning, with a lot of missteps along the way.

3. **Get excited about discovery.** There are very few experiences in life that are better than the excitement of discovering something new.

4. **Remember that science is self-correcting.** There may be something you think is one way, but if you really delve into it, you may reveal that it's another way.

5. **Keep learning.** Science can expand who you are. The more you learn, the more insight you have into everything about yourself, the people in your life, and the world you live in.

TIME LINE

As director of the National Institute of Allergy and Infectious Diseases, Dr. Anthony Fauci has advised seven US presidents on health issues. Here are some milestones from his life.

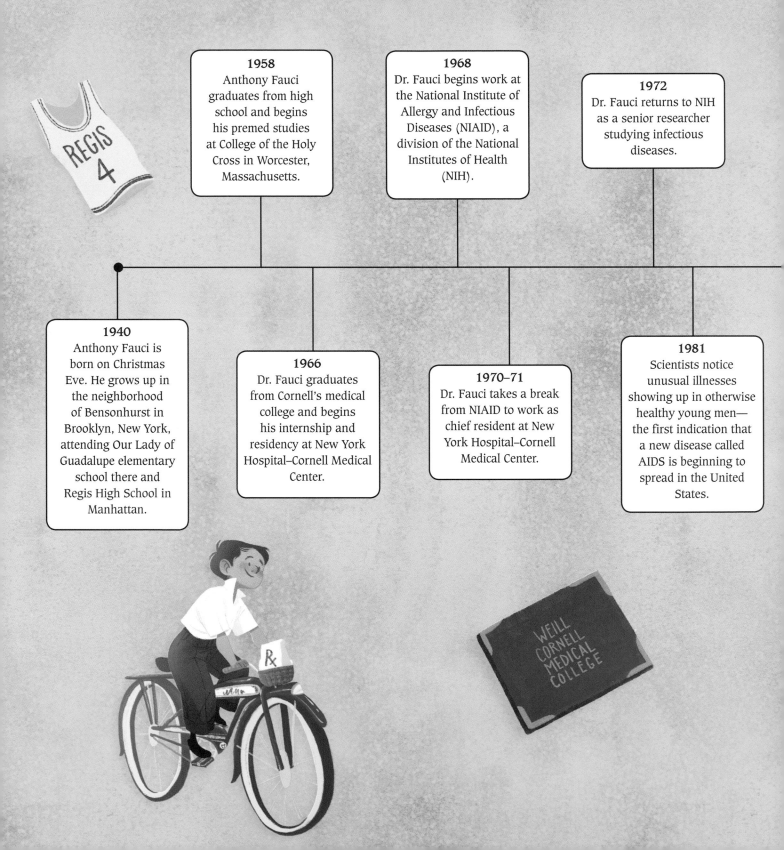

1958
Anthony Fauci graduates from high school and begins his premed studies at College of the Holy Cross in Worcester, Massachusetts.

1968
Dr. Fauci begins work at the National Institute of Allergy and Infectious Diseases (NIAID), a division of the National Institutes of Health (NIH).

1972
Dr. Fauci returns to NIH as a senior researcher studying infectious diseases.

1940
Anthony Fauci is born on Christmas Eve. He grows up in the neighborhood of Bensonhurst in Brooklyn, New York, attending Our Lady of Guadalupe elementary school there and Regis High School in Manhattan.

1966
Dr. Fauci graduates from Cornell's medical college and begins his internship and residency at New York Hospital–Cornell Medical Center.

1970–71
Dr. Fauci takes a break from NIAID to work as chief resident at New York Hospital–Cornell Medical Center.

1981
Scientists notice unusual illnesses showing up in otherwise healthy young men— the first indication that a new disease called AIDS is beginning to spread in the United States.

1984
Dr. Fauci becomes director of NIAID, where he studies AIDS and other infectious diseases.

2003
Dr. Fauci works with President George W. Bush to create the US President's Emergency Plan for AIDS Relief, which invests billions of dollars to fight AIDS around the globe.
Dr. Fauci also works with other researchers to study and contain the spread of a new respiratory disease called SARS.

2014
An Ebola epidemic breaks out in West Africa and spreads through travel to several people in the United States. Dr. Fauci helps treat an American healthcare worker who was infected overseas, and he works with other scientists to contain the outbreak.

1999
A new disease called West Nile virus is identified in the United States. Dr. Fauci and other scientists lead an effort to combat the outbreak.

2008
Dr. Fauci is awarded the Presidential Medal of Freedom for his work fighting infectious diseases.

2020–2021
A new disease called COVID-19 emerges and quickly develops into a pandemic. Dr. Fauci serves on the White House Coronavirus Task Force, working with other public health experts and scientists toward the goal of ending the outbreak.

Here are some books to explore if you'd like to learn more about infectious diseases, the germs that cause them, and the scientists who have studied them.

All in a Drop: How Antony van Leeuwenhoek Discovered an Invisible World by Lori Alexander, illustrated by Vivien Mildenberger (New York: Houghton Mifflin Harcourt, 2019)

Cells: An Owner's Handbook by Carolyn Fisher (New York: Beach Lane Books, 2019)

Do Not Lick This Book by Idan Ben-Barak, illustrated by Julian Frost (New York: Roaring Brook Press, 2018)

Germs: Fact and Fiction, Friends and Foes by Lesa Cline-Ransome, illustrated by James Ransome (New York: Henry Holt and Company, 2017)

Germs Make Me Sick! by Melvin Berger, illustrated by Marylin Hafner (New York: HarperCollins, 2015)

Germs Up Close by Sara Levine (Minneapolis: Millbrook Press, 2021)

History Smashers: Plagues and Pandemics by Kate Messner, illustrated by Falynn Koch (New York: Random House, 2021)

It's Catching: The Infectious World of Germs and Microbes by Jennifer Gardy (Berkeley: Owlkids Books, 2014)

The Polio Pioneer: Dr. Jonas Salk and the Polio Vaccine by Linda Elovitz Marshall, illustrated by Lisa Anchin (New York: Alfred A. Knopf, 2020)

Science Comics: Plagues: The Microscopic Battlefield by Falynn Koch (New York: First Second, 2017)

A Shot in the Arm! (Big Ideas That Changed the World #3) by Don Brown (New York: Amulet Books, 2021)

Tiny Creatures: The World of Microbes by Nicola Davies, illustrated by Emily Sutton (Somerville, Massachusetts: Candlewick Press, 2016)

SOURCES

Academy of Achievement. "Anthony S. Fauci, M.D." Revised March 4, 2020. https://achievement.org /achiever/anthony-s-fauci-m-d/#interview.

BBC. "Anthony Fauci: The Face of America's Fight against Coronavirus." BBC News, July 13, 2020. https:// www.bbc.com/news/world-us-canada-52027201

Bernard, Diane. "Three Decades before Coronavirus, Anthony Fauci Took Heat from AIDS Protesters." *Washington Post*, May 20, 2020. https://www.washingtonpost.com/history/2020/05/20/fauci -aids-nih-coronavirus/.

Centers for Disease Control and Prevention. *Understanding How Vaccines Work.* Updated July 2018. https://www.cdc.gov.

Cohen, Ben. "Dr. Fauci Was a Basketball Captain. Now He's America's Point Guard." *Wall Street Journal*, March 29, 2020. https://www.wsj.com.

Fauci, Anthony. Email interview with the author, May 27, 2020.

Fauci, Anthony. Zoom interview with the author, November 23, 2020.

Gallin, John I. "2007 Association of American Physicians George M. Kober Medal: Introduction of Anthony S. Fauci, MD." *Journal of Clinical Investigation* 117 (October 1, 2007): 3131–3135. https://doi.org/10.1172/JCI33692.

Grady, Denise. "Not His First Epidemic: Dr. Anthony Fauci Sticks to the Facts." *New York Times*, Updated March 11, 2020. https://www.nytimes.com.

Lamb, Brian. "Q&A with Dr. Anthony Fauci." C-SPAN, January 8, 2015. https://www.c-span.org/video /transcript/?id=9390.

National Institute of Allergy and Infectious Diseases. "Anthony S. Fauci, M.D., NIAID Director." Accessed January 26, 2021. https://www.niaid.nih.gov/about/director.

Office of NIH History & Stetten Museum. "Anthony S. Fauci, M.D." In *In Their Own Words . . . NIH Researchers Recall the Early Years of AIDS*. National Institutes of Health. https://history.nih.gov /display/history/Dr.+Anthony+S.+Fauci+Transcript.

Specter, Michael. "How Anthony Fauci Became America's Doctor." *New Yorker*, April 10, 2020. https:// www.newyorker.com.

Unger, Donald N. S. "I Saw People Who Were in Pain." *Holy Cross Magazine*, Summer 2002, vol. 36, no. 3. https://www.holycross.edu/departments/publicaffairs/hcm/summer02/features/fauci.html.

US Department of Health and Human Services. "Vaccines Protect Your Community." Reviewed February 2020. https://www.vaccines.gov/basics/work/protection.

World Health Organization. "How Do Vaccines Work?" December 8, 2020. https://www.who.int.

Zimmer, Carl, Jonathan Corum, and Sui-Lee Wee. "Coronavirus Vaccine Tracker." *New York Times*. Accessed December 5, 2020. https://www.nytimes.com.

Sunday dinner with Anthony's grandfather

Anthony's father, sister, and Anthony

AUTHOR'S NOTE

Quotes from Dr. Fauci's grandfather and father are based on Dr. Fauci's recollections of those conversations, as shared with me in a Zoom interview on November 23, 2020.

ACKNOWLEDGMENTS

I'm most grateful to Dr. Fauci for making time to be interviewed for this book, and to the NIAID staff who offered assistance as well. Many thanks to Greg Folkers, Patricia Conrad, Kim Barasch, and David Awwad for their kindness and patience in scheduling interviews, coordinating technology, responding to emails, and answering my questions, even as they were hard at work dealing with the COVID-19 pandemic response.

Anthony with his high school basketball team

Anthony

Anthony, age seven

For all the scientists, health care professionals, first responders, and essential workers.
Thank you.
And for the scientists and problem-solvers of tomorrow.
Dream big.

—K. M.

For my hardworking friends Jessie, Rachel, Elaina, Colby, and Tyler.
I'm so proud of you guys and all that you do to help people be well.

—A. B.

Anthony's parents at their pharmacy

Anthony in his first year of medical school

All family photos courtesy of A. S. Fauci.

DON'T GET discouraged. THINK ABOUT IT carefully. Try TO WORK IT OUT.

Fauci PHARMACY